Forex for Beginners

The Ultimate Guide to Profitable Currency Trading

Gualtiero Favole

© Copyright 2021 by Gualtiero Favole. All right reserved.

The work contained herein has been produced with the intent to provide relevant knowledge and information on the topic on the topic described in the title for entertainment purposes only. While the author has gone to every extent to furnish up to date and true information, no claims can be made as to its accuracy or validity as the author has made no claims to be an expert on this topic. Notwithstanding, the reader is asked to do their own research and consult any subject matter experts they deem necessary to ensure the quality and accuracy of the material presented herein.

This statement is legally binding as deemed by the Committee of Publishers Association and the American Bar Association for the territory of the United States. Other jurisdictions may apply their own legal statutes. Any reproduction, transmission or copying of this material contained in this work without the express written consent of the copyright holder shall be deemed as a copyright violation as per the current legislation in force on the date of publishing and subsequent time thereafter. All additional works derived from this material may be claimed by the holder of this copyright.

The data, depictions, events, descriptions and all other information forthwith are considered to be true, fair and accurate unless the work is expressly described as a work of fiction. Regardless of the nature of this work, the Publisher is exempt from any responsibility of actions taken by the reader in conjunction with this work. The Publisher acknowledges that the reader acts of their own accord and releases the author and Publisher of any responsibility for the observance of tips, advice, counsel, strategies and techniques that may be offered in this volume.

Table of Contents

Introduction 9

Chapter 1: Introduction to the Forex Market . 11

  What is the Forex Market? 12
  Types of Forex Markets...13
    Spot Market 13
    Forward Market 16
  Factors Affecting the Forex Market.......................19
    Political Landscape of a Country........................20
    Inflation..21
    Interest Rates...22
    Government Debt 22
    Country's Current Account 23
    Terms of Trade..24
    Speculation 24
  Forex Trading vs. Stock Trading 25
    Leverage 25
    Liquidity...26
    Paired Trades 27
    Trade Activity and its Effect on Price.................28
    Market Accessibility..29

Chapter 2: Fundamental and Technical 31

Analysis in Forex 31

  Fundamental Analysis 31
    Tools...33
    Indicators...34

    Advantages & Disadvantages 38
  Technical Analysis 42
    Tools 44
    Advantages & Disadvantages 46

Chapter 3: Basic Forex Trading Strategies That You Should Know 51

  Breakout Trading 52
  Moving Average Crossover 53
  Trend Following Strategy 55
  Using Trendlines 58
  Carry Trade 59
  Momentum Trading 61
  Range Trading 62
  Using Purchasing Power Parity Indicator 63

Chapter 4: Tips For Acquiring the Right 67

Trading Mindset 67

  What is a Trading Mindset? 68
  Why is it Essential For You to Have a Positive Mindset? 70
  Here Are Some Tips to Groom Your Mindset 72
    Always Keep Learning 74
    Never Let Losses Dictate Your Actions 75
    Learn to Adjust to the Market 76
    Don't Overwhelm Yourself 77
    Be Persistent 77

Chapter 5: Money and Risk Management to Avoid Losses 79

Trade With Capital That You Can Afford to Lose..82
Don't Chase the Market..83
Learn to Quantify the Money You Are Risking in
Each Trade...84
Design a Good Trading Plan.....................................87
Cut Your Losses Short 89
Set a Risk-Reward Ratio 90
Use Limits and Stops..92
Be Careful About Leverage 93
Don't Forget Currency Correlations.......................94
Keep Emotions in Check 95

Chapter 6: How to Create a Trading Plan?....99

What is the Need for a Trading Plan? 102
Steps to Create a Successful Trading Plan 103

Conclusion 109

Introduction

Congratulations on purchasing *Forex for Beginners,* and thank you for doing so.

Did you know that the Forex market witnesses a $4 trillion trading volume every day? There are so many people who are investing in the Forex market, so why shouldn't you? You simply need a good internet connection and some basic knowledge to start, and in this book, you will be introduced to the concepts of Forex trading that will help you get started and make money. You don't even have to leave your day job if you want to invest in Forex. You can simply do it in your spare time. Start with a minimal sum, and you should practice with a demo account.

Once you read this book, you will have a comprehensive idea of how everything works here. You will get introduced to the main players and also figure out why the Forex market is so fascinating to everyone around the world. You will also know more about trading plans and strategies and how to have one for yourself. The Forex market has been there in existence for years, but now, it has become so popular mainly because of the presence of electronic trading, which has made the Forex market available to all. By the time you reach the end of this book, you will be ready and geared up to make your first trade.

There are plenty of books on this subject on the market, thanks again for choosing this one! Every effort was made to ensure it is full of as much useful information as possible, please enjoy!

Chapter 1: Introduction to the Forex Market

Before we go into the details of Forex trading, you need to have a basic knowledge about the Forex market, and that is exactly what we are going to do in this chapter. Forex or foreign exchange is being traded 24 hours every day for five days a week by institutions, banks, and individual traders all over the world. Another thing about Forex is that it does not have any centralized marketplace. So, at any point in time, whichever market is open, currencies are traded over-the-counter.

Thus, Forex is a global marketplace, and here, different national currencies are exchanged against each other. Finance, commerce, and trade have a worldwide grasp in today's world, and because of this, Forex is often considered to be the most liquid and largest asset markets around the globe.

What is the Forex Market?

The place where all the currency trading is done is termed as the forex market. People might not realize it that often but currencies are important to everyone irrespective of the country they live in. This is mainly because, in order to conduct business or foreign trade, the currency has to be exchanged. You, as a common civilian, might understand the importance of currency when you are traveling to a different country, for example, Thailand. If you are from the US, US dollars will not be accepted in Thailand. You have to exchange your US dollars into Thai baht, and only then can you purchase things there.

The major centers in terms of the forex market are
Zurich, Tokyo, New York, London, Hong Kong, Frankfurt, Sydney, and Paris. Now, as we said before, the forex market is open all day. When the trading day is coming to closure in the US, in Hong Kong and Tokyo, the forex market begins. Thus, there is no particular time in the day when you can say

for certain that the forex market will remain highly active. It stays active any time of the day, and there is a constant fluctuation of the price quotes.

Types of Forex Markets

When broadly classified, there are two main markets in the foreign exchange category, and they are – spot market and forward market, and we are going to learn more about them in detail.

Spot Market

Among the different types of markets in Forex, here, you will find the quickest transactions. According to the present exchange rate, both sellers and buyers will get instant payment in this type of market. In fact, one-third of all the transactions happening in the forex market is part of the spot market, and for settling the transactions, usually 2-3 days are required by the traders. And because of this, the traders can stay open to the currency market's volatility. As a result of this, the price can either become less or rise between the trade and the agreement. When the deal of the currency is closed by the buyer and the seller within 2 days from the date of the deal, it is called a spot transaction. The spot exchange rate is referred to the rate at which the settlement of the transaction is done.

In the forex market, the volume of such spot transactions has increased a lot. These transactions usually happen through banking system transfers, cash-in of traveler's cheque, and trading of currency notes. But the most common one is the banking system transfer, which accounts for about 90% of the total transactions. These are specifically carried out by different banks.

Now, let us have a look at some of the main participants of these type of transactions –

- **Commercial Banks** – The first participant, which is also the main player in the spot market, is the commercial banks. This is because investment and commercial banks trade both for their customers and themselves. In fact, they aim at making a profit from exchange movements, and thus, the currencies put in by the bank are what make up the maximum portion of the transactions. If the volume of the transaction is huge, then the interbank transaction is also done. But when a small volume is involved, it might be done with the help of a broker.

- **Central Banks** – To reduce the fluctuations of the currency of a particular country, the central bank of that country will intervene in the foreign exchange market. Their aim is to ensure that the national economy's requirements and the exchange rate of their currency are compatible. In fact, the central banks might release some foreign currency into the market so that their own currency does not undergo any further depreciation. The appreciation of their currency is reduced by doing the reverse.

- **Brokers and Dealers** – Selling at high and buying at low are what dealers do. They are mainly involved in wholesale purchases, and in fact, they mostly perform interbank transactions. They might even deal with central banks and corporates from time to time. They have a very thin spread, and the costs involved in the transaction are quite low. As far as the overall value of deals in the forex market is concerned, 90% of them are wholesale transactions.

Forward Market

In the case of the forward market contract, a future date is decided by two entities or parties when the trade will be made at a stated quantity and price. When the deal is signed, there is no exchange of money, and so, no amount of security deposit is required. The trade is usually made after 90 days of the deal signing date.

Now, you might be wondering whether this type of contracting has any advantages or not.

Well, there are some that you should know about – for starters, these types of contracts are mostly used in case of speculation and hedging. There are speculators in the market who study everything, perform thorough research, and then use that information to predict whether there will be an increase in the price. Then, if they do speculate that there will be an increase, they buy currencies in the forward market instead of buying in cash. After that, they would simply wait, and if their prediction is correct and the price increases, they would sell the currencies at a higher price, thus bringing home a handsome profit.

But along with these advantages, there are some disadvantages too. I have tried to explain them as concisely as possible –

- There are no centralized rules when it comes to trading in the forward market.
- Since only two parties are involved here, it is highly illiquid.

> o   The risk of default is always present, and so, there is counterparty risk.

In the first two problems that I have mentioned above, the presence of a lot of generality and flexibility is the main problem or point of concern for traders. It's like dealing with a real estate contract when only two persons are present. These two persons who are involved in the deal are the only ones who get to decide the terms of the contract based on what is convenient to them. If any of the two parties that are involved in the transaction declared bankruptcy, the other party would suffer, and this is known as counterparty risk, which is always present in the case of the forward market.

Another major point of concern while trading in the forward market is the time span and the fluctuations in that time span. The more the time span for which the contract is open, the greater will be the risk of huge movements in price. Thus, the counterpart risk present in the transactions keeps increasing.

Factors Affecting the Forex Market

The fluctuations and variations in the currency exchange rates that you see happen because of several factors that directly or indirectly affect the forex market. They lead to volatility, and if you want to enter the forex market, you need to know about these factors. Now that Forex has become a global marketplace, all the macroeconomic events happening across the world have a direct impact on the forex exchange rates. With modernization, you don't really have to remain concentrated on the popular currencies, but for someone who is starting out, the popular currencies are a good option. Overall, it is safe to say that any new information or current events can quickly affect the economic health of countries, and thus, the exchange rates. Below are some of the popular factors that you should keep in mind.

Political Landscape of a Country

The currency strength of any country is hugely affected by its economic performance and its political state. If political turmoil is less likely to happen in a country in the upcoming days, then foreign investors would be more interested in that country. This would mean that there would be an influx of foreign capital into that country, which, in turn, would lead the domestic currency to follow the path of appreciation. When the trade policy and financial condition of a country are in a sound place, they do not usually allow for any amount of uncertainty in their currency. But the exchange rates will witness frequent depreciation in the case of countries with political confusions.

When the government is willing to take the necessary steps to improve everything in a country, the economy will automatically flourish. Thus, investors look for countries that have a stable government because they know that such countries have a much higher chance of growth, and there would be very few roadblocks in their way. For example, when news of Brexit came out, the GBP suffered a dive in price compared to USD.

Inflation

I think this one shouldn't be of that much surprise because if there is something that lays a direct impact on the currency, then it is inflation. The currency value of a country will follow the path of appreciation if the inflation rate of that country is lower than that of the others. When the rate of inflation is low, there is a slow increase in the prices of different things. Similarly, if the rate of inflation in any country is high, then it's currency will follow a path of depreciation. Now, for an investor, a currency whose rate of inflation is lower would be attractive. For example, there was an aggressive devaluation of the Zimbabwe currency when the country went through a period of serious inflation, and so, in the forex market, the Zimbabwe currency does not hold an attractive place.

Interest Rates

The value of a currency and its exchange rates depends largely on the interest rates. Inflation, interest rates, and forex rates are three entities that are all interrelated. The currency of a country follows the path of appreciation when there is an increase in the interest rate because lenders get higher rates, which means there will be more influx of foreign capital.

Government Debt

The national debt or the public debt that the Central government owes is referred to as the Government debt. Foreign capital is not likely to enter a country that has a huge amount of government debt and this, in turn, leads to a rise in inflation. If a country has government debt, then the bonds will be sold in the open market by foreign investors. Thus, it will lead to a subsequent decrease in the exchange rate value.

Think of it in this way – if someone who already has a lot of debt comes to you asking for money, would you be willing to give it? No, right? The same thing is happening here. The government debt of a country over the past couple of years is studied by foreign investors before they decide to part with their money.

Country's Current Account

When a country makes a foreign investment, there is a balance of trade and earnings, both of which are reflected in the current account of the country. All the transactions of debt, imports, and exports are included here. Depreciation of the exchange rate happens when the country is not earning a sufficient amount through the sale of exports, but at the same time, it is spending huge amounts of money on importing certain products. The domestic currency exchange rate fluctuates depending on the balance of payments.

Terms of Trade

In simpler terms, the terms of trade are nothing but the ratio of export prices to that of the import prices. If the rate of increase in export prices is way more than that of import prices in a country, then there is an improvement in terms of trade. The direct result of this is that the revenue of the country improves. Thus, the value of the currency of that particular country also increases, and the currency is now high in demand. Thus, the exchange rate follows a path of appreciation.

If we see from the point of view of an investor, then they would be more interested in those countries which have lesser imports and more exports.

Speculation

Among all other factors, this is not really something that you can measure. The rate of a currency increases when there is speculation of its rate to increase in the coming days. Investors from all around the world will flock to the currency. But the catch here is that you have to identify this trend and also be out of it in time because if you stay inside it for too long and the trend ends, then you will be the one at a loss.

So, these were some of the factors that you should know about if you are planning to enter the forex market as they affect the exchange rates of different currencies.

Forex Trading vs. Stock Trading

Forex leverage is the first and foremost reason why so many people prefer forex trading over stock trading. In this section, we are going to discuss that, along with several other points.

Leverage

As far as stock trading is concerned, 2:1 leverage is used by the margin account traders. Although you have to keep in mind that people who perform day trading can also access leverage of as much as 4:1 because they open their positions and close them on the same day provided that their account balance is above $25,000. Apart from this, the 4:1 leverage can only be accessed once you have met a few other criteria as well. A margin account is not given to every investor, at least not right away, and in the case of stock trading, if you want to leverage, a margin account is mandatory.

But, let us come to forex trading – here, you do not need a margin account. If you want to use leverage in trading, you simply open a forex trading account. There are no requirements to be met. The leverage amount differs from one country to another. In USA, a 50:1 leverage is what your limit is, but there are countries where it can be leveraged to as much as 400:1.

Liquidity

As you might already know, in stock trading, you are basically buying the shares of different companies. The cost of these can vary a lot. It can be as low as tens of dollars to even hundreds of dollars. Demand and supply are what determines the price of these shares. But in the world of Forex, things are quite different. Yes, there are chances of fluctuation in the exchange rate of a country's currency, but even then, you will have a huge amount of currency at your disposal that you can use to trade. And this is why currency as an asset is highly liquid.

Paired Trades

The quotation for currencies in trading is always done in a pair. Thus, it simply means that you have to think about both countries and their economies – the country against whose currency you are trading and the country whose currency you have chosen.

The market also determines what you should be concerned about. Let us say that you have purchased Intel shares, then your main concern is not what is happening to other companies and their shares but whether or not there will be a rise in the value of the stock you hold. But if you see the scenario of the forex market, you have to be concerned about the economies of the countries whose currencies you are trading. Does one country have better political stability than the other? Does one of them have a better GDP or more job growth? These are the things that you will have to think about. Thus, there are two financial entities that you need to worry about when you are trading in the forex market and not just one.

Compared to stock trading, Forex is usually more sensitive to economic and political situations in other countries.

Trade Activity and its Effect on Price

The price sensitivity of the stock market with respect to trade activity varies greatly from that of the Forex market. The stock price might be impacted when 10,000 shares are purchased, especially when small companies are concerned. But for greater companies or giants like that of Apple, this would hardly scratch the surface.

On the contrary, the market price of the currency will not be affected even a bit even when there are a hundred million dollars of forex trades.

Market Accessibility

In comparison to stock markets, greater access is provided to the currency markets. Well, if we are to see the modern-day, then it is possible for you to trade stocks all throughout the day (24 hours) and for five days a week, but as far as the difficulty level is concerned, it won't be easy. But due to the presence of several forex exchanges spread across the world, you can do forex trading 24 hours a day and for six days a week with ease.

And lastly, the regulations will give you much more freedom in the forex market than it will give you in the stock market. But at the same time, it is these regulations in the stock market that give you a certain amount of protection that you cannot get in the forex market.

Chapter 2: Fundamental and Technical Analysis in Forex

When it comes to market analysis, there are two major types that you should be aware of – technical analysis and fundamental analysis. These two options are not mutually exclusive, but if you talk to any trader around you, everyone will fall into one of these two categories.

If we were to judge them from a neutral standpoint, I'd say that both have their own share of drawbacks as well as advantages. Here, in this chapter, we are going to learn more about both these types of analysis in detail.

Fundamental Analysis

If you want to make correct predictions as to whether the currency exchange rates are going to up or down, one of the methods of evaluation is termed fundamental analysis. The main idea behind fundamental analysis is that you have to study and do research about various macro-economic events and then figure out how they are affecting a particular currency. You also have to keep an eye on the social and political news and any monetary policy shifts. You have to make this analysis for both currencies in the currency pair.

Let us say that you are working with a regional currency, for example, Euro – in that case, you have to analyze the entire regional economy along with the member states so that your evaluation of the financial status of the region turns out to be accurate.

In short, whenever there are some changes in the geopolitical or economic nature of a country, currency pairs react at once. This reaction can turn out to be even more drastic when the change occurs in a way that was not initially expected. That is why a fundamental analysis of the market is of utmost importance so that you can understand the changes that are going to happen in the exchange rates in the near future and in which way the market is going to move.

Tools

Now, let us see what the different tools that are used in fundamental analysis in the forex market are. Firstly, there is historical data, then comes financial news from different types of media, and then there is the economic calendar.

The factors that can leave an impact on a national currency, be it any minor economic data or a major one, will be informed to the trader through the economic calendar. You will get to know the time and date of these releases. The financial news broadcasts that are done on various types of media will tell you whether there have been any major geopolitical event or any other economic change that you should be concerned about.

And then there are historical fundamental data through which you will get to know whether there was a similar economic situation in the country in the past and how the currency had reacted in that situation at that time.

Indicators

In this section, we are going to discuss some of the major indicators in the fundamental analysis that will help you understand whether a potential change in the exchange rate is coming or what the overall strength of the economy currently is. In fact, some of these indicators are so powerful and important that they might even be able to tell whether the economy is going to turn down or turn up any time soon.

So, let us see some of these important indicators in the forex market in more detail –

- **Trade Balance** – As I explained to you in the first chapter, the trade balance refers to the difference between the total exports and the total imports of a country. This particular indicator has a direct effect on the currency of the country and whether it is in demand or not. If the trade balance is more and there is a surplus, then it means that the

country is doing good because the amount of imports is less
than that of exports. On the other hand, if the trade balance is less and there is a deficit, then it means that the country is not performing well and the number of exports is less than that of the imports.

- **Employment Reports** – This refers to all kinds of data related to jobs – for example, the total number of claimants or applicants for a particular service, the unemployment rate, and also the levels of payrolls along with several other important things.

- **Current Accounts** – All the net cash transfers and balance of trade of a particular country are shown in the current accounts. If this amount shows a deficit, then it means that the country is neck-deep in debt. But if the amount is in surplus, then it shows that the total debts of the country are less than that of the total foreign assets.

- **GDP** – This stands for Gross Domestic Product, and the currency of a country depends largely on this value. The economy of a country is presumable in a good and stable state if there is an increase in GDP value, and this would also mean that the currency of the country would follow the path of appreciation. This is even stronger if there is a possibility of an increase in interest rates.
- **CPI** – This stands for Consumer Price Index, and this indicator is very important with respect to inflation. It acts on the consumer level and shows at what level the prices of different products are. The central banks of any country are highly focused on controlling the rate of inflation, and so, the monetary policies of the country can be influenced by CPI. The interest rates would increase when the rate of inflation increases, and at the same time, the interest rates would hit a low when the consumer prices are low.

- **PPI** — Before a finished product is made, the amount that the manufacturers are paying in order to get their raw materials is denoted by PPI or Producer Price Index. Now, you must be wondering how this affects the currency of a country. Well, it does, because higher consumer inflation in the future is indicated by a higher PPI value and vice-versa.

- **National Credit Quality** — There are major agencies around the world that give ratings to countries based on whether they have defaulted on their loans or they have the intention to repay them, and this will indicate the credit quality of that country. This would have a direct impact on the currency of the country.

- **Commodity Prices** — Next, we come to another important indicator that plays a vital role in identifying disinflationary and inflationary cycles in both consuming and producing nations. Let us take crude oil, for example. If the price of crude oil decreases, then the first impact would be on transport, and thus, the different goods' costs would also be influenced. The level of inflation would also be reduced. But the inflation would rise if the price of crude oil were to increase.

Advantages & Disadvantages

Now that you have a basic idea of what fundamental analysis is all about, we are going to check some of its advantages and disadvantages.

The advantages are –

- **Explanation of Price Movements –** Movements in price can happen very quickly, and as a beginner in the world of Forex, you might not always understand what is happening, and that is where fundamental analysis comes in. It will help you keep up with the economic reports and news, which are the major reasons behind price movements. The movements are even drastic when there is some unexpected economic change.

- **Finding Valuation** – There is a specific value for every asset or financial instrument. So, you as a trader will have to go through these values, and if you find that the current market price and the true value of an asset have discrepancies, then it is your job to find that out. The fundamental analysis gives you the scope of going through industrial production, consumer sentiment, inflation, interest rates, and so on, all of which help you to find out asset values.

- **Understand Global Markets** – Lastly, the fundamental analysis makes it easier for you to get a grip on the international markets. No matter what country is concerned, you will understand its economy in a glance if you know how to perform fundamental analysis.

The disadvantages are as follows –

- **Overload of Information** – The most obvious disadvantage that you are also going to feel is that fundamental analysis sometimes provides you with so much information that you feel overloaded. In fact, for a beginner, it can be quite overwhelming, and you might even miss out on the important bits amidst such chaos. Thus, the entire process becomes counterproductive.

- **Absence of Market Timing** – When it comes to exits and entries, fundamental analysis cannot really help you – yes, it will give you a broad insight but not such minute technicalities, which are equally important.
And you must know that timing is the holy grail of trading – you cannot afford to go wrong there. Thus, in order to

know when you should enter or exit a particular trade, you have to use technical analysis along with fundamental analysis.

- **Not Meant for the Short Term** – Another grave drawback is that even though you will get the fundamental data of the economy on a monthly basis, it won't really help you in the short-term. There will be a lot of spikes owing to huge volatility.

- **Subjective to a Great Extent** – Yes, there are concrete reasons for everything in fundamental analysis. But an analyst who thinks the price is going to move in a certain way believes so because of a lot of probable reasons, and similarly, an analyst who believes quite the opposite will also give you several believable and concrete reasons.

Technical Analysis

To put it in a gist, we use past movements in price to perform technical analysis. In fact, you will often hear analysts saying that this type of analysis involves less science and more art. Do you know why? It is because sometimes there are nuances occurring in between, mainly because the entire concept of technical analysis relies on predicting price movements based on past data. Thus, sometimes, conclusions might not be the same.

Price data is the first and foremost tool that is used in technical analysis. This is a very important consideration, and it doesn't matter what timeframe you have chosen for this. In fact, you will be provided with a framework through technical analysis that will help you to compare the present data to other historical occurrences of a similar type and study the present price action in detail.

Before we proceed, there are three very important things about technical analysis that you should know —

- Every technical analyst has the belief that the market participants can know everything that there is to know from the current trading price itself. Even if there is some new piece of information, the trading price would quickly reflect it.

- The market always follows certain trends. And if you notice the price changes in a market with a trained eye, you would be able to spot these trends. And these trends are often very much predictable.

- The market has always shown a tendency to repeat history. Thus, trends are of a recursive nature. But I must warn you about something — even though history repeats itself, the trend might not appear in the exact same way as it did before. There will be some resemblance, but there will also be some newness to it.

Tools

Now let us have a look at some of the common tools used in technical analysis —

- **Forex Volatility Tool** — This tool functions in a specific time period by providing the traders with a pip range. The range of periods could be anything like a week or a day, and the range is the average in that time period. You will be able to set a proper target profit range when you know for certain what the volatility of your currency pair is.

- **Currency Correlation Tool** — Sometimes, there is a relation between the price movements of a currency pair. Suppose a currency pair is moving in the same direction, then the correlation is said to be positive. Similarly, if the currency pair is moving in the opposite direction to each other, then the correlation is said to be negative. When a trader follows a currency table, it becomes easier for them to notice and keep track of such relationships. Knowing these things will help you in better risk assessment and management of the same.

- **Price Action Analysis** – The balance between demand and supply in the market is identified through the price, and so it is a very important tool. In fact, there are traders who trade solely on the basis of price action analysis. They identify the movements in price through the use of candlesticks.

- **Oscillators and Technical Indicators** – This is one of the most popular tools used by technical analysts. There are several types of indicators included under this one, like Bollinger bands, RSI, MACD, Keltner channels, and so on.

Advantages & Disadvantages

Here are some of the advantages of technical analysis –

- **Can Be Done in Any Time Frame –** Whether you are trading in the long-term or short-term, technical analysis will be fruitful in all types of time frames.

- **Takes Market Timing Into Consideration –** Unlike fundamental analysis, you can detect your entry and exit from the market with the help of technical analysis. It will tell you when is the best time for executing a particular trade, and everything will be done in an efficient and methodical manner.

- **Helps You Analyze Trends –** Technical analysis uses different types of tools for detecting and studying different market trends. For example, support and resistance, swing highs and lows, moving averages, and so on.

- **Less Overwhelming** — Since there are a lot of things in fundamental analysis, it often gets tiring and overwhelming. But that is not the case with technical analysis because here, everything is a lot more simplified. Price action is the primary variable everywhere in technical analysis, and so things are less complicated.

Now, let us look at some of the disadvantages —

- **Might Give You Mixed Signals** — One of the major drawbacks of technical analysis is that sometimes you might get mixed signals from the different indicators. For example, you might be getting a buy signal from one of the indicators, and at the same time, some other indicator might signal you to sell. This can get you confused and frustrated, and you might end up making the wrong decision.

- **Your Biases Might Influence It** – Technical analysts often get swayed by their biases. For example, if you have a bullish bias, then you might end up overlooking the several signals that point in the opposite direction. And the worst part is that you won't even realize that this is happening to you.

- **Chances of Overanalyzing** – Since there are plenty of technical tools that are available to you in today's world, you might end up overanalyzing the situation, and it would only lead to confusion. You won't be able to take a distinct trading decision.

So, I know you might be wondering what to choose – technical analysis or fundamental analysis? Well, it depends entirely on you, but I would suggest you to use a mix of both. But remember that there is no right or wrong answer here. You simply have to use a particular approach and then see whether it works for you or not.

Are you enjoying this book? If so, i'd be really happy if you could leave a short review on Amazon, it means a lot to me! Thank you!

Chapter 3: Basic Forex Trading Strategies That You Should Know

There are countless trading strategies that you can pursue in the world of Forex, but for traders who are just beginning in this world, the most common question is that which strategy should they use? Well, we are going to answer that question in this chapter by providing you with some common and easy strategies. These strategies are the ones you should always keep in your toolbox, and soon, you will realize that they have become a staple in your trading journey.

Once you have mastered these basic strategies, you will become more confident and also become ready to tread onto more advanced grounds.

Breakout Trading

The first strategy that we are going to discuss is something that all of you should learn no matter what. It is also quite easy and simple to grasp, especially for someone who is just starting out. But before we go into the details, I want you to specifically understand what the term 'breakout' means.

In very simpler terms, when there is a movement of price outside of resistance or support areas, then it is termed as a breakout. It is referred to as a bullish breakout when there is an increase in price that goes beyond resistance areas. And then, there are bearish breakout patterns wherein the price decreases below the support areas.

But do you know why this strategy is considered to be so important? Well, the primary reason is that when you identify a point of breakout, it also signifies that the market is going into a very volatile stage. And if you are quick enough, then you can even put this volatility to your advantage by identifying a trend when it begins and joining it.

Your aim should be to enter early and keep riding the trend until there comes the point where the volatility starts to die down. And your stop loss will then have to be placed at a point that is either below or above the breakout candle.

Moving Average Crossover

In this strategy, the average price will be updated constantly so that the price data is smoothed out. The time period of this average can be anything. It can be as much as 30 weeks or 30 minutes – it entirely depends on what you are choosing. The best thing about this strategy is its ability to be tailored to any time frame you want, thus making it appropriate for both short-term and long-term traders.

One of the main reasons why traders prefer this strategy so much is that it helps you in identifying both resistance and support levels.

Traders who love to follow technical analysis get the signal when the price of the asset goes beyong the particular moving average.

Now, let us talk about a simple price crossover – among the different trading strategies that involve the moving averages, this is the most common one. When the price of the asset crosses either below or above the moving average, that is when the simple price crossover happens. This means that the trend is about to change.

There is another common strategy used by traders where they implement two moving averages. One moving average is shorter while the other one is longer. A buy signal is generated when the shorter moving average crosses the longer moving average and goes above it. This indicates that the price trend is moving upwards, and so you must sell the asset. This is also known by a popular term – golden cross.

Another variation of the above-mentioned strategy is when it generated a sell signal. It happens when the shorter moving average crosses and goes below the longer moving average. The indication is that the trend in price is moving down. This type of crossover is also referred to by a special name – death cross or dead cross.

Trend Following Strategy

These strategies are perfect for newbies in the forex market. You simply have to observe the market very closely for any changes and patterns. You have to spot a trend assuming that the trend will keep going on in that same direction. There are several reasons why you should be using this strategy. For starters, they are very easy to identify. But before you act on the trend, you need to confirm it. If you think that trading on the trend means that you have to spot when the market is down and buy, and vice-versa then you are wrong. It means that you have to spot the exact time when the market seems to be on the verge of going up, and that is the moment when you need to buy.

Here are some indicators and how they will help you spot these trends emerging

- **Bollinger Bands** — These are most helpful because they assist you in identifying the volatility of the market. You can find out whether the market is in an uptrend or downtrend. You will know that the market is very volatile if the bands are situated at a point that is quite far away from the present trading price. And similarly, it means the opposite when the bands are located very close to the current price. Both these situations should be avoided even more so if you are a beginner. Bollinger bands are mostly used in this way — when the price reaches the upper band, you
sell, and when the price reaches the lower band, you buy.

- **Moving Averages** – You already know about moving averages – they help you in finding the direction of the trend. But what you need to keep in mind is that this indicator will not inform you whether the trend is coming to an end or not, and so relying only on them would be a wrong decision. When the present trading price goes below the moving average, you buy, and when it peaks at the moving average or goes above it, you sell.
- **Relative Strength Index (RSI)** – You will understand whether an asset is underbought or overbought with the help of this indicator. An asset is said to be underbought when the RSI is below 30%, and it is said to be overbought when the RSI is above 70%. If there is no change in price and yet the RSI decreases, then you might predict a downtrend. So, before the downtrend actually starts, you need to sell. But relying on RSI cannot be done solely. You have to use other indicators to confirm the signals.

Using Trendlines

This is another simple yet effective strategy that you should learn. You simply have to join two price points (two highs or two lows) on the trading chart with the help of a line. If we assume that there is always some sort of trend in the forex market, then the trendlines will help you identify in which way the trend is moving – is it going up or is it going down? Sometimes we do not recognize certain economic effects or price movements on the charts with our bare eyes, and the trendlines help to identify those.

But if you have been noticing the price to bounce off the same trendline repeatedly, keep in mind that you are not the only one seeing it – others are too. It is true that this type of situation will help you get a few good entries one after the other, but you also have to keep in mind that the trendline won't be there forever. So, before it fails, you need to have your stop loss ready.

There are different tools that are used by traders following the trend trading strategy, and some of them are stochastics, directional indices, volume measurements, RSI, and moving averages. All of these will help you identify and evaluate the trends.

Carry Trade

This is a very specific type of forex trading. When you are dealing with different currencies belonging to different countries, there is often an interest rate difference, and if you can put this difference to your advantage, then that is what carry trade is all about. But at the same time, I'd like to bring to your notice that this type of forex trading can be extremely risky.
However, it is quite popular too.

The basic principle of working of this strategy lies in the fact that the currencies are bought in one day, and then they are held overnight. In this way, the trader gains profit from the interbank interest rate. The catch is to select a country that will give you a lower rate of interest and buy the currency from them so that you can then fund your next purchase – which will be a currency with a higher rate of interest than the previous one. Amazing, isn't it? The difference between these two rates is what will give you the profit. The amount of leverage that you are using will determine how much profit you are making, and mind it; it can be a substantial amount!

Out of all the strategies in the world of forex trading, you will find that this one is quite popular, but as I told you before, it can be quite risky too, and the main reason behind it is that there can be overcrowding because of excess leverage.

But here are some common trading pairs for this strategy – New Zealand dollar/Japanese Yen and Australian dollar/Japanese Yen. These pairs are usually used because the spread of the interest rates in these pairs is quite high and can be used to your advantage.

Momentum Trading

Another very popular strategies used by traders in the forex world is momentum trading. The price trends in recent times are used by traders to buy currencies and then sell them.

Let us say that a trader is implementing the momentum forex trading strategy and if he sees that the price of an asset has started moving in a particular direction; then they make a bet that the direction of movement will remain unchanged.

There are certain aspects of trading that are used to define momentum – for example, the rate of a price change or trading volume. In fact, did you know that research shows, when we are talking about high volumes, there is always that one stock in the market every day that can move up by as much as 30%? This hugely depends on certain announcements and news releases, so you must definitely not miss out on them.

So, the main idea behind momentum trading is that when traders see a strong movement in price in a certain direction, they are of the belief that the price will keep moving in that direction for a certain period of time. Similarly, if you consider the opposite, they like to believe if a movement has weakened, then it means that the trend is most likely to die down. Tools that involve visual analysis like candlestick charts and oscillators are usually used by traders in momentum trading.

Range Trading

Now let us talk about another popular yet very simplified trading strategy of the forex market – range trading. The assumption on which this strategy is based is that prices of currencies when considered within a limited time period, stay within a fixed price range. But this type of trading strategy would be advisable to use only if the economy is predictable and, most importantly, stable. You also have to be sure of the fact that there are no surprise news events coming up that could cause a dent in your plan.

Traders who follow the range trading strategy buy and sell currencies very frequently, and they do so at rates that are highs and lows of resistance and support. In fact, they might even repeat it in a single trading session.

There is a similarity of the tools being used between range traders and trend traders when it comes to fixing an exit and entry point. These include stochastics, commodity channel index, and relative strength index.

Using Purchasing Power Parity Indicator

If you are in search of trading strategies that would be profitable and, at the same time, not too difficult to use for you as a beginner, then using Purchasing Power Parity levels and comparing the exchange rates with them would be a good option.

Now, if you are wondering what the Purchasing Power Parity indicator is, well, it helps you to identify the rate at which the average prices of different services and goods can be equalized. So, you can say that a currency is undervalued if it has been trading at a price that is lower than the PPP. Similarly, a currency is overvalued if its exchange rate is higher than the PPP.

But don't get me wrong. Just because you have decided to follow the PPP indicator for forex trading doesn't mean that the market will do the same at all times. However, if you are considering the major currencies, you will notice that their trading range remains within the 20% range, give or take.

This strategy is very popular among beginners because of its ease of use, but there is something that you should keep in mind – the strategy works best when you are considering trades with a longer time horizon. But if you are considering a shorter time span, for example, a daily basis, you will notice that the exchange rates vary widely, and they keep diverging from the PPP levels by huge numbers. And the balance is not restored any time soon – it can even take weeks for that.

So, now that you have learned about all the major strategies for beginners, the trick to picking the right strategy for yourself lies in choosing the appropriate level of risk management, good money, and leverage. If you do not follow all the basic principles, then no matter how good your strategy is, you will still suffer from huge losses.

If you want to become a professional at forex trading, you have to hone your skills and form good strategies. You also need to have a trading plan about which you will learn in the latter part of this book. Once all of this is in place, you can slowly move on to the more complex strategies. Maintain realistic expectations and enjoy what you are doing.

Chapter 4: Tips For Acquiring the Right Trading Mindset

Developing the right mindset for trading is essential to be successful, but people often fail to realize that. Fear of making mistakes or losing money will be your greatest enemy when it comes to trading, and that fear can be overcome by honing your skills and working on your mindset. Trading psychology is a subject that is widely studied by researchers around the world. It deals with the fact that you need to modify your personality so that you can keep a check on your emotions and not let them mess with your head while you are trading.

Being a successful trader is not only about doing an extensive analysis of market stats or coming up with better strategies; it is also about building the right trading mindset. But most beginner traders believe that only if they can get their hands upon that perfect strategy they can make substantial amounts of profit. But that's not how things work – it's not so easy. If all you needed was a well-formed strategy, then all of us would have been billionaires by now. There are people who have good strategies and yet keep losing huge chunks of money every day.

And there are some traders who have been consistently doing well in the forex market because they have achieved that psychologically right mindset, and that is what differentiates winners from losers.
The world of forex trading needs you to have certain psychological characteristics, attitudes, and beliefs that will help you make more money and be successful in forex trading.

What is a Trading Mindset?

Before I give you some tips on improving your trading mindset, you need to understand what a trading mindset truly is. You have to understand that there is no morality or emotions associated with the market. So, let us say that you want to continue trading in the long run and want to make some substantial profits from it, then you have to form the right mindset for it too, and this can happen once you learn how you can observe the market without being emotionally attached to it.

All your actions ultimately depend on what mindset you carry. You can either make huge profits or suffer huge losses depending on the mindset you have. And even if you do suffer from a loss, the right mindset will prevent you from giving in to the panic and help you make decisions with a sane mind. You cannot afford to base any of your decisions on your emotions, and that is what trading psychology is all about.

A trader who leads a disciplined life will never let anything come in between their trading decisions. But it is not easy to become a disciplined trader, and more importantly, it does not happen overnight. You need to put in an equal amount of effort, willpower, and time and then you can become the disciplined trader you need to be to make successful trades.

Why is it Essential For You to Have a Positive Mindset?

Like you already know – there are no emotions associated with the market – the only emotions at work are those of yours – the market participants. This is also the reason why the different trendfollowing techniques and charting patterns work out brilliantly. They are primarily based on market psychology and human behavior that are predominant.

I don't know whether you have heard of this famous phrase or not, but there is a saying that within 90 days, 90% of the trading funds or 90% of traders will be lost. That means that the successful traders of the market account for only 10%, so what is it that sets them apart? The answer is a positive mindset, and in this chapter, you will learn how you can build one.

There are some traders who are of the belief that the market and everything else is somehow rigged against them – this type of negative mindset hinders their growth. If your thoughts and decisions are clouded by such opinions, then you will never be able to analyze the market from an objective point of view. You have to keep in mind that the market doesn't care whether you win a lot of money or you lose everything – it is completely neutral in that sense.

Thus, if you notice or talk to any of the successful traders or read their interviews, there is one thing that you will find common in every one of them – selfconfidence. They have a belief in their abilities and in themselves, in general – this type of positive mindset and outlook is important. No matter how many trades you lose, this belief should not be shaken.

On the other hand, traders who keep losing all the time often have this looming self-doubt troubling their minds. They think that bad luck follows them all the time or they are cursed or whatever. And with time, this erroneous belief somewhat turns into a self-fulfilling prophecy. When you are not sure about your own decisions or abilities, you will hesitate to take action or initiate trades when you should have, and in this way, you miss out on profit-making opportunities. There is no use in being overly fearful of everything when it comes to trading, and you need to understand this right from the start.

Yes, it is true that sometimes the movements in price cannot be explained by even the best market analysis, but you have to acknowledge and respect that and not blame it on the market being out to get you because there is no such thing as that.

Here Are Some Tips to Groom Your Mindset

A relaxed and calm mindset is what you need to ace at trading. You also need to implement the right risk management strategies, which you will learn in the next chapter. For now, what you need to understand is that even if you lose a trade or two, it's not the end of the world for you. Even the most successful traders in today's world have lost trades, and this happens all the time. Let us say you manage to keep up a winning rate of 50% and your reward-to-risk ratio is set high enough, then you will be able to take home handsome amounts of profit. So, instead of focusing on winning all trades, what you should do is focus on each trade at a time. If you lose, learn from your mistake and try again. If you win, don't consider yourself to be someone who will neve make any mistakes. Stay humble and keep trading.

Also, you need to learn not to take things personally when you are trading. A trade gone bad is just what you see it is – a trade gone bad. There is nothing to be personal about it. The market might not perform in the same way every day, and so, you simply have to implement everything that you have learned and keep faith in the market analysis that you are doing.

So, here are some tips that will help you work on building a trader's mindset and win more trades.

Always Keep Learning

Remember that there is always something new to learn in the world of trading. There are newer strategies, newer modes of analysis, and so on. You need to be a student forever. In fact, one of the most important factors that set a successful trader apart from an unsuccessful one is educating yourself more and more about the trading world and forex markets. This book will help you form a foundation that will get you started, and if you follow everything that I have mentioned here, you will have a comprehensive overview to keep trading.

Education about forex trading is what will help you understand certain market reactions and hence, the price moves. In this way, you will be able to make better predictions. There are endless concepts that you can learn in the world of forex trading. There is literally no end to the list, but what you need to do is figure out which one of these concepts or strategies work the best for you, and then, you need to keep honing your skills and that strategy with time.

There is one thing that you can do to make learning a habit – pick a trading book and promise yourself that you are going to read it at least for an hour before you sleep or any other time of the day when you think you have time. This is a practice that many of the wellknown and successful traders encourage beginners to do. You can also try several trading courses that are now available online.

Never Let Losses Dictate Your Actions

There is a common tendency among beginner traders to let emotions cloud their judgment whenever they lose trades. In fact, there are some traders who believe that they always need to close in a win, and thus, they keep trading and making the wrong decisions even when the market requires them to do the opposite. So, do you see how emotions from losses can hamper your trading career?

You have to learn to cut your losses short. If you see that one of your trades is not performing the way you expected it to, don't wait. Get out of it and minimize your losses. You need to move on to better trades and not keep losing money on the same trade.

Learn to Adjust to the Market

The conditions of the market are not going to be the same at all times. Today the market might be performing well, but in a few weeks, months, or days, it might completely flip from its current position and start going in the opposite direction. You have to be equally flexible and accommodate these changes in your strategy. Maintain your views at a neutral point and then analyze the market. If your analysis says that it is time to change your direction of trading, then you need to do so. Don't let any preconceived notions or emotions overrule your market analysis. Never hesitate to trust your research.

Don't Overwhelm Yourself

There will be times when everything gets messy, and the market is all over the place, and your original strategy no longer holds for the current scenario. Regardless of what is happening around you, you have to maintain an objective outlook. This is what will make you disciplined as a trader. If the market seems to be too chaotic to handle and you think you are not ready for it, don't stress too much and wait for the dust to settle. When you notice a signal that you do recognize, you can then seize the day. Whatever trading strategy or setup you choose to follow, it must have become like a second nature to you by now. If you are planning on taking up a new setup, then practice it in market conditions that you are habituated in. Once you have become a master in that trading setup, only then use it in crisis situations.

Be Persistent

Lastly, I'd like to remind you that no one became a successful trader overnight. It takes time, patience, and experience to become an expert at something. Just because you faced a few losses doesn't mean that you will quit and leave. Take it as a learning experience – let your mistakes teach you something.

Keep a journal where you will note down all your trades, for example, your entry and exit points or why you chose to enter that trade in the first place. You can also jot down some additional comments that you want your future self to remember.

You will identify a lot of trading patterns from your journey by maintaining a trading journal. It will help you improve your skills.

So, now that you have read the chapter, I want to remind you that if you seriously want to be a successful trader, you cannot sit on your couch and procrastinate. You have to get up and put in some actual effort. As we all know that every trade comes with its share of risks, and risk management is an equally important part of being a successful trader, which is what brings us to our next chapter.

Chapter 5: Money and Risk Management to Avoid Losses

In this chapter, I am going to give you a crash course on how you can minimize your losses and maximize your profits in forex trading through the right strategies of money and risk management. Many beginners think that if they have figured out the direction of price movement in the forex market, then they have won the trade, but that's only one side of the coin. The other side comprises risk management. Trading in the forex market always has a lot of risks, and if you cannot take steps to manage that risk, you are going to lose money one way or the other.

Traders, especially the newbies, have the habit of neglecting this aspect of trading; however, it is not a clever thing to do. But if you want to become successful in trading, there are a few risk management rules that you have to keep in mind, and we are going to learn those rules in detail in this chapter.

Before we move on to the rules, I want to introduce you to the common types of risk that you will be dealing with in the forex market.

- **Interest Rate Risk** – This is also the risk that is a result of volatility. Volatility in the market is what leads to abrupt changes in interest rates. When you consider the whole economy, there is a change in the amount of investment and spending, which changes the foreign exchange rates.

- **Currency Risk** – Then we come to the currency risk whereby the prices of currencies undergo a fluctuation causing the currencies to become less or more expensive when it comes to purchasing foreign assets.

- **Leverage Risk** – This applies to those traders who are trading on a margin because they stand a chance of experiencing losses that are hugely magnified. The value of the forex trade, in this case, is much bigger than the initial outlay, and so, beginner traders often forget how much amount they are leaving at risk.

- **Liquidity Risk** – This is when you want to prevent a loss, but you cannot do so because you cannot sell or purchase the currency as quickly as you need to. Yes, I know that I have told you at the beginning of this book that one of the advantages of forex trading is its high liquidity, but there might be certain scenarios when there is illiquidity. This mostly happens because of the release of certain government policies that suddenly changes the playing ground for everyone.

Trade With Capital That You Can Afford to Lose

The first and foremost tip for managing your money and limiting your risk is to trade only with that amount of money that you can afford to lose. It's quite simple, really. You need to deposit a certain amount of money to your trading account, right? So, this amount should not be more than what you can afford.

To make the process easier, evaluate the expenditures that you have every month. And then, think about it long and hard and then set a particular value that is acceptable to lose for you in a month. You have to make a note of the fact that if you have already touched this level, then you need to stop trading at all costs. The main aim of this tip is that you should not be risking an amount of money that could drastically turn your life upside down if you happen to lose it. Thus, a rule of thumb is not to put your money for essential needs into trading. This includes the money you need every month to pay for your mortgage, rent, commutes, food, other bills, and so on. Remember that even though trading can earn you quite a fortune, it's not a guaranteed money-making machine. So, you will be making a lot of mistakes and lose some money before you learn to trade successfully. Thus, don't lose any money that you cannot afford to part with.

Don't Chase the Market

Now, let us discuss the next most important thing in forex trading – you have to resist the urge to chase the market. When someone is new in the world of forex trading, they do not understand the risks associated with chasing each and every trading opportunity. Some of them might not have sufficient chances of winning, and when you chase such a trade setup, there are high chances that you will end up with a big loss. Newbies are often excited to have their new trading account, and being in the forex market that they overlook other important factors. They even place more than one trades within an hour just because they think one of them is bound to bring them profit, but things don't work that way. If someone exercises this type of behavior, then it is more like gambling and less trading.

You have to keep it in your mind that there is nothing that is owed by the market to you. In order to be a successful trader, you need to have a lot of patience, and with time, you will understand that even more. For example, if, on a particular day, you do not find sufficient solid trading opportunities, you need to take a step back and wait for your entry the next day. Chasing the market will not bring you anything. No matter how much profit you have made, never forget that a single losing trade is enough to take away everything you won.

Learn to Quantify the Money You Are Risking in Each Trade

In the first point, I already explained that you should not be trading with the money that you need for your day-to-day essentials. So, once you have figured out the amount of money that you are going to put into your trades, it is time that you also figure out the sum that you are risking in each trade. But why do you need this? Well, figuring out the risking value will help you set the stop loss. Quantifying your risk can be easily done, and there are two methods from which you can choose –

- **A Fixed Percentage** – The first method is the most common one whereby you maintain a fixed percentage of your trading account balance that you are going to risk in every trade. So, let us assume that the balance in your trading account is $10,000, and you have decided to quantify your risks at 2%, then every trade that you make will be risking an amount of $200. So, what is the advantage of using this process? It will ensure that even if you lose a trade, the whole account balance is not lost. Moreover, the higher the amount of trading capital you possess, the higher you can risk in any trade because you have set it at 2%. But there is also a

disadvantage to this method. If someone has suffered a setback of losses one after the other, then there will come the point where their account balance has diminished a lot, and the amount of money they have left or
they are risking is very low. The direct result of this is that winning back the money you lost will also take you quite some time.

- **A Fixed Sum** – Another school of thought is that you should set your risk limit per trade at a fixed amount rather than a fixed percentage. For example, a trader might decide to risk $500 in every trade when they have deposited an amount of $10,000 in their trading account. The rule is not too hard to keep in mind or follow. The advantage is that you know exactly how much amount of money is at risk for each trade. So, if you decide to make a total of five trades a day, no matter what, the total amount of money you stand to lose is $2,500 and not more than that. But the disadvantage with this system is that you risk $500 in every trade irrespective of how much you have in your trading account. At the same time, if your trading account balance has increased to a great extent owing to some consecutive wins, you will not be risking much and thus, miss out on greater returns just because you thought of risking only $500 in every trade. On the contrary, if you have lost a maximum portion of your money and you have only $2,000 in your account, in that case, risking $500 in every trade means risking a substantial portion of your total trading account.

Design a Good Trading Plan

You can make your forex trading experience way easier only if you have a well-designed trading plan with you. It will act as a guide to help you make decisions while trading. In fact, if the market becomes volatile, making the right decisions at the right time can be tricky, but a good trading plan can make it easier and also encourage discipline. If your trading plan is built the right way, then it should answer your questions of when, what, how much, and why you are trading.

Every trading plan is different. The main idea behind building trading plans is that they should be made somehow personal to you, having your own ideas and your personal touch. If you want to just copy someone else's trading plan, it will not help you in any way. The main reason behind this is that the person whom you are copying might not have the same goals as you. Their ideas and attitudes might not match yours, and so, their trading plan is not going to work for you. Another significant difference between your trading plan and that of others is the amount of money you are ready to risk in trading – it might not be the same as that of the other person.

Lastly, I'd like to remind you of the importance of maintaining a trading journal or a diary – this will help you keep a record of all the trades that you are placing and all strategies that you are implementing. You should even note down your emotional state during each trade. We will cover the topic of building a trading plan in detail in the next chapter.

Cut Your Losses Short

A rule of thumb followed in all forms of trading – be it forex trading or any other type of trading – is that you have to cut your losses short. In simpler terms, if you notice that one of your trades is not performing well and things have not panned out the way you thought they would, then the losses from your trade will keep accumulating. In that case, you have to close the trade as soon as you can. Similarly, when your trade is performing well, you need to keep it running but only up to a certain point. You need to fix a stop loss and not be too greedy – you never know when everything changes. Stay aware of the conditions of the market so that you can get out of the trade at the right time and bring home huge profits.

Traders who have just begun often don't follow this rule. When they start losing money in a trade, they think that keeping it open is the best thing to do so that they can wait for the course to eventually run in the opposite direction. Similarly, they sometimes exit out of profitable trades too soon because they fear losing out on money. Greed and fear are two of the most dangerous emotions to fester in the world of trading. If you want your trading career to grow, you need to let go of these emotions.

Set a Risk-Reward Ratio

In the previous steps, you have learned that you need to set a fixed amount of money that you are willing to risk in each trade. Once that is done, the next step is to figure out how much profit you are aiming to make in the next trade. That level will mark the take profit level for each trade.

Your aim of profit will largely depend on your profile of trading and the strategies that you use. And most importantly, it is your risk appetite that will determine your profit-taking mark.

Now, let us assume that you have set your risk to reward ratio at 1:1 then; that would mean, if your acceptable amount of loss is $200, then your profit target in that trade should also be $200. However, for someone who has a risk to reward ratio of, say 1:3, then they would have a target profit f $600 with the same acceptable amount of $200 as a loss.

The general rule of thumb in forex trading is that your ratio of risk to reward should be something that is greater than 1:1. Do you know why? This is because even if you lose two trades in a row and then win two trades in a row, you would have a net profit, but if the ratio was 1:1, then, in this case, your net profit would have been $0.

Use Limits and Stops

As you must have already understood by now, volatility is a common presence in the forex market. So, even before you open a new position during your trade, you need to have your exit points ready. There are different types of limits and stops that will help you out regarding this –

- **Guaranteed Stops** – These stops will ensure that you exit from the trade at the specific price that you have stated. In this case, the risk of slippage can be avoided.

- **Normal Stops** – Then there are normal stops – their main function is to find their position on their own the moment the market starts going in the opposite direction. But protection from slippage is not guaranteed here.

- **Trailing Stops** – The nature of these stops is such that they closely follow the positive movements in price, and whenever there is a move that works against you, the trailing stop will exit your position in the trade.

- **Limit Orders** – Here, the main aim is to set a take-profit level and then follow it. Once the profit has hit that level, your position will be closed.

Be Careful About Leverage

Using too much leverage during trading is one of the most common mistakes, especially among beginners. You need to understand that even though leverage allows you to trade more, it is essentially a doubleedged sword. It is true that you will be able to increase your profits by ten folds because of leverage, but it is also true that if things don't work out the way you wanted them to, then it is the same leverage that will cause you to lose ten times more money. Trading on leverage is the most tempting thing to do in the world of forex trading because it will allow you to keep increasing the volume of your trading account.

But, at its core, this is not how you should be trading.

The first thing to keep in mind as a trader is that you have to protect your capital. Always keep the downside of trade in mind when you open a position and before you think about your potential profit, think about your potential loss. To determine what your appropriate amount of leverage should be, there are several things that you should consider, for example, the size of your trading account, the stop-loss distance, and the risk-per-trade that you have determined.

Don't Forget Currency Correlations

We know that in the forex market, currencies are taken in pairs, and they are priced in that same manner. So, in order to become a successful trader in the forex world, you need to understand the correlation between these currencies.

In this way, you will be able to build a better Forex portfolio, and your overall risks are also reduced. Everything will remain in your control. But what does correlation mean? It means studying the changes in one currency that are caused by the change of price of the currency in the pair. The currencies will move in the same direction if there is a positive correlation between them. Similarly, they will move in the opposite direction if there is a negative correlation between them.

Keep Emotions in Check

In trading, beginners often let their emotions come in between their trading decisions, and that is something you cannot afford to do. Your emotions will be triggered by the high amount of volatility in the forex market, but you cannot let yourself get overwhelmed. Emotions like doubt, temptation, greed, fear, and anxiety will not allow you to see things from an objective point of view, and you will simply start thinking from your heart. But letting your emotions get the better of you will only affect your trade outcome negatively.

So, if you are just starting out, all the money and risk management tips that I have mentioned in this chapter should help you find the right path. Once you have made your trading decisions, it is also important for you to stick to them no matter what. And like anything else in the world, being better at trading needs more and more practice. You can start with a demo account if you are a complete newbie.

With a demo account, you can test your strategies and make mistakes without worrying about the risks involved. Demo accounts will give you the chance to trade with virtual funds rather than risk your actual capital and lose your money. In this way, you will slowly get a better grasp of things and understand how the forex market works. You can also back-test your strategies and your trading plan with your demo account and then figure out all those places where there is room for improvement.

It is okay to make mistakes, but it is also important that you learn from them and promise yourself not to make the same mistakes again. If you suffer losses, learn to take responsibility for them. Don't play the blame game and blame the market for your loss – you need to understand that it is only you who determines what happens to the money in your trading account.

Chapter 6: How to Create a Trading Plan?

What we mean by a trading plan is nothing else by kind of a guide, or a sort of a map to help the investor to take proper decisions regarding this trade and to highlight to him what are the risks, what are the profit points and to help him draw out a plan so that his business runs smoothly. A proper trading plan should ideally tell an investor what his objectives should be to reach that goal, what are the risks he might have to face, how much time will he need to get there. An ideal trading plan should technically also point out the most profitable entry and exit points for the investor and the correct position sizing rules.

The plan should ideally also point out the position sizing rules, risk management techniques, how he will find the trade, and how he will need to execute them in return. The correct time and conditions under which the investor can buy or sell securities and, most importantly what are the kinds of securities that need to be purchased in the first place should also be indicated by the plan. The kind of securities that should be dealt with and the nature and position of their management are also important information that should be provided by the trading plan.

Along with these, a trading plan, which is basically a management guide, should guide you as to how to develop a proper trading system. It is ultimately a well-drafted trading plan that will help the investor to work in the market with minimum problems, and thus, quite naturally, it needs to be well researched and well-drafted, and it should also ideally provide the investor with adequate space for making any changes or adjustments later so that any kind of emergencies can be met at short notice. Every investor is supposed to have some personal preferences, objectives, and his/her unique way of going about their work in the market. And hence, it is the trading plan that tells us about their unique approach and style which sets them apart from other investors out there.

An indispensable part of any financial transaction, a trading plan is something that is highly recommended by every expert to their next in lines as any serious investment is bound to be backed by a well made and well-thought trading plan. For everyone who is newly exploring this field should know from the very beginning that it is of utmost importance to create down a detailed trading plan at the onset of starting an investing plan. Those who are veterans in this field will already know that your trading plan should ideally have a summary of all the key points regarding every step you are going to take so that you can have a clear picture of what you are getting yourself into. Having a solid idea of what are the strategies you want to take will keep you ready for everything that is to come. So, all in all, your trading plan will make the entire process of forex trading much easier for you and will definitely make it a much more convenient initiative to take.

What is the Need for a Trading Plan?

Having a trading point is of utmost importance as it helps you to actually take the journey from theory to experience. From reading and learning about the entire trading and investment plan to actually practicing it in the real market, it is ultimately the trading plan that helps you actualize it. Doing anything without proper knowledge of it will only lead to numerous problems and impending disasters. But having prior knowledge about it makes it easier. No matter how much you read about trading and marketing, it will never give you your needed expertise. It's like learning driving, and getting a license is not enough. Unless you actually drive that car by yourself, on a busy road, you will never gain confidence. Similarly, unless you actually draw up a plan and start taking action, you will not gain enough experience to make any difference. Only by maintaining a proper plan will you get to know about your own limitations and strengths, and that will, in turn, help you take sensible actions.

Steps to Create a Successful Trading Plan

Till now, we discussed what a trading plan is and why it is so very important to have a detailed trading plan before you start forex trading. Now that we have successfully established the importance of having a plan let us now discuss how to actually formulate a plan in real life. We understand that at times it might be a little too daunting but fear not. We have you covered. Down below, I am listing some easy, comprehensible steps to make a trading list that will help you understand the process with much ease so that you can develop your skills further.

- **Understand your skills -** This step is primarily for you. It's about you to ask yourself whether you want to actually trade or not. Then go ahead to ask yourself what kind of trading you want to go forward with. What are the risks you are comfortable in taking, what you think your strengths are, and how much do you think you can deal with? After you get these answers from yourself, you are ready for further planning.

- **Preparing yourself** - After you have your thoughts clear regarding your wants and expectations, it is highly important to prepare yourself both physically and mentally for what is to come. It is highly advisable not to neglect any physical needs like proper food and rest prior to the day of trading, as you will need all your strength. Simultaneously, if there is anything disturbing you mentally, it is advisable to deal with it before so that you have nothing to distract you on that day.

- **Fix your goals** - Both for beginners as well as for those with experience, it is very important to have a clear picture of your risk/reward ratio. You should have a practical idea regarding what your goals are. If you start with extremely ambitious goals, it might so be that you find it extremely hard to reach that goal for the first time.

What will happen as a result is that you might get demotivated to take further actions. But this shouldn't be the situation ideally. So, in the beginning, it will always be advisable to wrap your head around the actual practical picture and set yourself goals that you will not have much difficulty in reaching. Once you know what you want, it will be much easier to work accordingly so as to get that.

- **Set an upper limit for your risk level** - It is necessary for you to understand that no matter how much invested you are mentally with a certain trade, if you can estimate that it is going up above the risk limits you can handle, then you need to reform your strategies or in extreme cases, change your plans altogether. You simply can't let yourself go beyond a certain risk level. So, set yourself a limit. Anywhere between 1% to 5% is all right. If whatever trade you have taken up remains within this limit, it means that you can rearrange your strategies if any emergency. Anything beyond that means you need to rethink the trade before going ahead with it.

- **Do your homework well** - Before you start
with anything, it is absolutely necessary to do a thorough background check on everything that is related to your project. Get to know whether the currencies you want are up or down, do your research well both for your domestic and international market. Don't forget to run a check on all the data regarding economic policies. This is one of the most important parts of your entire trading process, as a huge chunk of your trading policies will depend on these market analysis and data, so you absolutely need to get these correct.

- **Prepare your trade well** - You need to select a method that suits you best in order to keep track of your trade journals. Once you have decided how to keep track of your trade, you now need to label what you think are the minor and major resistance and the support levels. After that, set yourself a convenient alert for all your entry and exit points.

- **Set the rules for entry and exit -** Both entry and exit points are of prime importance in any trade, so you really can't prioritize one over the other. Plan them ahead so that no problems arise later. You need to analyze your profit targets and breakeven points for setting the rules of your entry and exit points. What this will do is also help you by giving you an additional option B, in case things go wrong with your option A.

- **Maintain your records properly -** After
  you have collected all your data, your task is to maintain that and keep that updated. Mark out what your long-term and short-term strategies are. This will be your guidebook for handling any situation.

- **Analyze your performance** - Your trading plan will be your best critique as it will give you a clear picture of all your past and present trading actions, giving you a clear picture regarding how your future trades should be. It will make you learn from your mistakes and help you increase your future profit margins.

Conclusion

Thank you for making it through to the end of *Forex for Beginners*; let's hope it was informative and able to provide you with all of the tools you need to achieve your goals, whatever they may be.

There are so many people who start trading in the forex market each and every day. It's not difficult to start. All you have to do is do some research and take the first step. And if you have reached this page in the book, then you are ready to take that first step. With the boom of the internet, forex trading is no longer complicated. In fact, it has become more accessible and convenient. Forex trading has been growing significantly over the past few years, and now, it is time that you put your skills to good use and make money.

But I'd strictly advise you to first make a plan. Don't jump in right away. Make a plan and stick to it no matter what. In trading, the slow and steady wins the race. As you keep placing each trade, you will learn something new about the market. With time, these lessons will give you more success. Make the best use of a demo account because it will help you practice trading in an environment that mimics the market and yet is risk-free, which, in simpler terms, means that you are not losing any money here.

Finally, if you found this book useful in any way, a review on Amazon is always appreciated!

Remember to follow Gualtiero Favole on Amazon to not miss the next updates on the books in publication.

www.ingramcontent.com/pod-product-compliance
Lightning Source LLC
Chambersburg PA
CBHW071421210526
45465CB00001B/485